9-19-21

alyssa,

a gift for you

Be Happy always

your friend

Randa

THE SPIRITUAL AWAKENING OF H

RAMANDA

SCIENCE of MIND taught me how to pray...

I prayed for Christ Consciousness and joyous synchronicity...

& my life changed FOREVER!

Title:

The Spiritual Awakening of H

Author:

Ramanda

Published by:
Reflections of Divinity
Carmel, CA, USA

ISBN 978-0-9814861-0-9

Printed in USA

DEDICATION

Dedicated to the forward thrust of the
consciousness of humanity.

CONTENTS

CHAPTER 1

The Spiritual Awakening of H 1

Coming Home to Religious Science 1

My First Asilomar Retreat 3

The Beginning of Unusual Occurrences 3

My Extraordinary Experience at Asilomar August 4-10, 1985 . . 7

CHAPTER 2

Day One 11

Arrival at Asilomar 11

Prayer Treatment 12

CHAPTER 3

Day Two 15

Demonstration: My Boots 16

Reflection on Consciousness and Aging 17

Experiencing Self as Source 19

Reflection on This Day 23

CHAPTER 4

Day Three 25

The Partner's Heart Workshop 27

The Power of Our Thoughts and Words 28

CHAPTER 5

Day Four 31

Recollection 32

The Tree Branch 33

Experience of the Fog 35

Hugging a Tree 38

Food for Thought 39

Mysterious Feathers 40

Evening Calling 41

Vision Corrected 44

CHAPTER 6

Day Five 45

Ask and It Shall Be Given 45

Discovering the Meaning of Sustenance 47

The Alpha and Omega 49

CHAPTER 7

Day Six 51

Divine Dining 52

The Stump that Couldn't Be Reached 55

Oak That Wishes to Be Undisturbed 58

Last Night in Merrill Hall 59

Evening Adventures in Monterey 61

The Acquaintance with Colorful Language 63

The "Heavy Metal" Bar 64

CHAPTER 8

Conference Last Day 67

Conference Summation Gathering 67

The Universe Responds Again 69

CHAPTER 9

The Journey Continues. 73

   Synchronicity of Lights 73

   The Power of "I Love You". 74

   My Return from Asilomar 75

   Synchronicity in My Corporate Job 77

   Uncovering My New Name 78

   The Violet Flame 80

   Visions of Violet 82

   Mission Ranch, Carmel, California Sunday, November 23, 2008 . 84

   My Dear Friend, Mission Ranch December 8, 2008 86

CHAPTER 10

Reflections 89

CHAPTER 11

My Gift to You 91

   Consciousness 95

CHAPTER 12

Afterword: One Religious Science 99

   ABOUT THE AUTHOR. 103

Forward

How many times have you heard the phrase "stop and smell the roses"? At some point in our lives, we get caught up in the hustle and bustle of living. We were told that being busy and multitasking was vital to being a success. Race consciousness created something called the rat race and we joined in and kept going just like the treadmill at the gym. We often fall into the trap of consumerism and materialism.

The Spiritual Awakening of H is a reminder and a wayshower of returning to the One. There is nothing to acquire. Everything required is already within us simply awaiting our awakening. Ramanda shares his story in an easy-to-follow conversation. This book illuminates the beauty of listening to the calls of Spirit and taking the time to be fully present in the moment. There is beauty, joy, peace, magic, and sacredness all around us and in us.

With the backdrop of the majestic Asilomar Grounds in Pacific Grove, Ramanda takes us on a walk toward personal enlightenment. We are reminded to truly look at nature, look into people not at them, share ourselves with others when the calling urges us to do so. Ramanda also gives us permission to embrace silence and be within ourselves fully. This lyrical adventure is a serene and empowering read that will transport the reader to wherever they truly desire to be. The lessons are simple for those who listen.

Treat yourself to the words, wisdom, and light which flow from Ramanda onto the page. The sacred space awaits all of us and this book is one way to open up and live a fuller life through applying metaphysical principles in our daily lives.

Reverend Linda Fisher

Acknowledgments

I especially want to thank my teacher and dear friend, Reverend Betty Jones who encouraged me "...to take time to smell the flowers."

I also thank my Aunt Maren for suggesting that I take notes of my Asilomar experiences. It was with these notes that I was able to create this book.

I thank the Reverend William Curtis who inspired me from the first time I heard his Sunday lecture.

The assistance and encouragement of my dear friend Reverend Scott Foglesong, Ph.D. is what brings these pages to fruition.

A special thanks to Judy Larry and Linda Ruoho for their assistance in the completion of the revised edition.

Preface

Prior to attending this Asilomar event I was deeply inspired by reading *Life and Teachings of the Maters of the Far East* by Baird Spalding. Two other readings that are important to me are *Science of Mind* by Ernest Holmes and *The Edinburgh Lectures on Mental Science* by Thomas Troward.

In this book, I am but remembering... bringing together... reconstructing... events, circumstances, and experiences that occurred while attending a Religious Science Conference at the Asilomar Grounds in Pacific Grove California, from August 4 through August 10, 1985.

As I write these memories, incidents, and feelings which are but gifts given to me in the moment, my deepest hope is that these words and thoughts express themselves to you in a way that inspires and opens you to experience and share your own awakening. If there is one thing I have learned through my spiritual journey, it is that each one of us is programmed with the consciousness to experience the Divine within.

In this light then, it is my hope that in reading these shared experiences, you will experience more of yourself, and together we will become one with the Spirit that has given forth this message.

CHAPTER 1

The Spiritual Awakening of H

Coming Home to Religious Science

I attended a Lutheran grammar school and high school and often felt that there was another interpretation of the Bible that I wasn't hearing or reading. Something was missing in the teachings I was receiving, but I had no idea what it was. I just knew what I was being told wasn't captivating me, wasn't reaching me in a way that made me feel excited, and longed for more. Consequently, once I was out on my own I took a break for twenty or so years from religious activities and endeavors.

I contemplated many times over the years that there must be another meaning or interpretation of the Bible than that to which I had been exposed. I would ask myself over and over again, "What is it?" Eventually, I came to a place in my life where I felt a longing to seek a spiritual community that fed my soul. Each Sunday, I would attend a different church in search of something that I could relate to and be inspired by at the same time.

One Sunday, I found myself walking up to join a church service held in the Community Center in the town where I lived in southern California. I was a little skeptical at first and I thought to myself, "Have you lost your mind, this place doesn't even have a steeple or a cross!" Once inside, I found the same thing to be true – no cross or other church-like icons. Ten minutes later, I was holding back tears. The feeling of coming home was over-whelming. I instantly knew that all the people present in that room had experienced similar feelings about religion to those I had kept locked up inside me for so long. What was being taught was Science of Mind, also known as Religious Science or Mental Science, published in the 1930s by Ernest Holmes – teachings I later learned were part of a larger movement of "practical Christianity" known as New Thought.

I was so inspired by the words of Reverend William Curtis who spoke that Sunday in Camarillo, California that my life changed from that day forward. No more than ten minutes into the service, I even contemplated that perhaps I could become a minister of this teaching!

I started taking classes immediately, simultaneously enrolling in the first two levels of Science of Mind. I remember being amazed when other class members commented how hard they had to apply themselves to grasp the material and do the homework. To me, it was as if I already knew all the teachings in that huge volume. Finally, I discovered people speaking my language!

My First Asilomar Retreat

The Beginning of Unusual Occurrences

It happened that I took part in my first Asilomar experience a few months after getting involved with Religious Science (now known as the Centers for Spiritual Living). Asilomar is a beautiful conference center located in Pacific Grove, California on the coast of Monterey Bay. The environment there is definitively coastal: boardwalks through sand dunes laced with delicate vegetation, roaring surf with jagged cliffs and boulders creating enticing coves, drifting fog with gusting breezes sometimes lasting the entire day, blazing blue magnificence when the sun does choose to appear.

Asilomar itself is a large conference center that is situated on 107 acres that is also a state park with a collection of architecturally elegant structures designed to harmonize with the landscape including the Administration building (a nice open gathering place), the large meeting space Merrill Hall, Crocker Dining Hall where all the meals are served, the Chapel (a quite spacious meeting area), several clusters of smaller meeting spaces and a range of overnight accommodations ranging from rustic to more modern.

At this first conference, my roommate was a gentleman who had just graduated from the ministerial course in Chicago, taught by Carlton Whitehead (who at that time was the President of this division of Religious Science). In the adjoining rooms on either side of us were other friends of his who had also graduated from the ministerial course.

It was such a delightful experience being around them. I will always appreciate and remember the way they guided me to pay attention to my words (and my thoughts!). Whenever I spoke something that pointed to an underlying limiting belief, they would suggest an adjustment to my sentence structure and choice of words in such a loving way that I never once took offense at their correction. I would say, "I can't..." and they would suggest a modification by saying, "You can...!" or "You have already...!" These interactions increased my awareness every time they happened! I am forever grateful to these people who shared so lovingly with me. The entire week I was (quite willingly) subjected to continual correction to frame my speaking in a positive way. This is the core of Science of Mind practice and I was blessed to be immersed in the teaching of these new ministers.

Those interactions set the tone for the entire week for me. And then, on the second day's session in Merrill Hall, I had an incredible experience that opened my receptivity to further adventures that were to come a few weeks later at my second Asilomar retreat (with the other division of Religious Science- the United Church of Religious Science).

As I sat in the audience looking at the presenter, the background behind him would fade away, turning into a cloud of white instead of the walls and curtains. When I would blink, the speaker appeared again with the walls and curtains behind him. As I continued to stare at the speaker again, the background was replaced by what appeared to be a white fog. That would fade away into a green forest of trees behind the speaker. When I blinked the walls and curtains appeared again behind him. "What's going on?" I wondered to myself.

I was sitting about a third of the way back in the auditorium, and curious as I was about what was occurring, I turned my head to look over my shoulder at the audience. I saw a white "fog" over the entire audience in Merrill Hall and as I looked back at the presenter, he said, "I'm looking out at you in the hall and I see above you this white cloud representing the unity of our consciousness." A chill of exhilaration erupted over my entire body, and I relished this extraordinary experience.

That was the beginning of many odd and synchronistic occurrences that took place throughout that week. I began paying close attention to every little thing that was happening, such as hearing a tune in my head and then hearing it on the radio seconds later. I began having "Aha!" experiences regularly.

Perhaps you have had a similar experience in your life: an energy that you can feel that starts at the base of your spine moves upward and vibrates in every nook and cranny of your body. Someone once told me that these goosebumps – or when the hair stands up on the back of your neck – are an indication of the increased awareness you are experiencing, in other words…your mind-expanding. Well, my mind must have really been growing while I was at Asilomar during this spectacular week, because I experienced that rush daily.

Toward the end of the week, I recall hearing one of the attendees bemoaning the fact that it was approaching time to return to our homes, saying, "This experience has been so incredible…it's too bad you can't put it in a bottle and take it with you." I thought, "That's not my truth. I know you can take this with you." How can something so life-changing be confined to this place? I have relived the lessons of that first Asilomar experience many times over the years. It was a stepping stone to my second and most extraordinary Asilomar experience that changed my life profoundly and permanently.

My Extraordinary Experience at Asilomar

August 4-10, 1985

After my return home from my exhilarating first conference at Asilomar, I attended the center in Camarillo, California again. The minister, during his Sunday sermon/ talk, made several references to the presentations at the retreat and he stated that he regretted having to wait a whole year until the next conference at Asilomar. Pondering this, I thought to myself that I wasn't going to wait a whole year. A few weeks later I attended the center in a different Religious Science church in Oxnard, California, and was delighted to hear the minister discussing plans for their upcoming Asilomar retreat! That is when I had another Aha! Moment. I knew that I didn't have to wait a whole year before attending another Asilomar Conference. That is when I first learned there were two divisions of the Religious Science

organization. I immediately signed up for the upcoming retreat, thrilled that I didn't need to wait a year to continue the magical experience I had just begun to open up to during my first retreat.

When my friend and guide Betty learned how excited I was to participate in a second retreat, she encouraged me to "take time to smell the flowers." My aunt Marne, who was a staff minister at a Religious Science center in the San Diego area, encouraged me to take notes on my experiences. Following the guidance of these two beloved persons, I permitted myself to engage in the retreat in my own way with total openness to the unexpected. And what an exquisite gift it was for me!

As many of you know, the western group of Science of Mind (now known as the Centers for Spiritual Living) was separated into two divisions. At the time of this revision, the two groups have merged into one organization after many years of negotiation. I have included more information in the afterword of this book.

CHAPTER 2

Day One

Arrival at Asilomar

I checked in at Asilomar and was assigned a room in a motel off the grounds. After unpacking, I spent some quiet time alone in my room. Relaxing in comfortable solitude, I began what is known as a spiritual mind treatment or affirmative prayer. That treatment set the tone for the experiences during the upcoming week and, as it turned out, for the rest of my life.

Treatment, as a key tool of the Science of Mind teachings of Ernest Holmes, is the art, the act, and the science of consciously inducing thought within the Universal Subjectivity, for the purpose of demonstrating that we are surrounded by a Creative Medium, which responds to us through a law of correspondence. In its more simple meaning, treatment is the time, process, and method necessary to the changing of our thought/mind. Treatment is clearing the thought/mind of negation, doubt, and fear, and causing it to perceive the ever-present God or Source within us.

Prayer Treatment

Beloved Father. All that you are, I AM   There is One Infinite Power, one loving Creator of all, and that loving essence flows through and around me. I am one with the creative essences of the universe, I AM, and Christ consciousness. I AM awakened to this presence in my life. Joyous synchronicity surrounds and flows through me. Every word I speak has power and authority. Every step I take allows me greater realization of that which I AM. I release and totally submit to this Divine action. With profound humility, thanksgiving, and joy I release these words and know that as I have spoken it, SO IT IS.

Slowing myself down, I let go of all thoughts. I gazed into a mirror above the dresser in my motel room and relaxed. I stared deeply into my eyes for several minutes as I began the treatment. Because I was so open and ready for this experience, I was not just saying some words, but I connected so deeply with the message in the words that I began to cry. I could not look into my eyes in the mirror without being overcome with emotion.

Each time I looked into my eyes in the mirror, and as I started to say the words of the treatment, a rush of such deep humility and reverence came over me that I burst into tears. This continued through the treatment. I had to stop many times and begin the thought over again after gaining my composure. As I came into eye contact with myself again, I would start crying as I spoke the words. I repeated the process five to seven times before I finally completed the treatment with my eyes closed. At its conclusion, I opened my eyes and began crying again as I looked at myself in the mirror. I know that I saw myself for the first time as who I really am. That moment was very humbling and lives with me daily.

As the profound experiences of the week unfolded for me, I asked again and again why these things were happening. I continued to attribute the events of the week to the depth of my connection with the prayer treatment that first day.

CHAPTER 3

Day Two

This morning I paged through the program of activities for the week – what I refer to as the "Hymnal" – that is folded and stapled together, with hymns at the back that we are invited to sing together at the sessions and events. As I looked through the Hymnal and studied the various activities, I recalled the "smell the flowers" guidance I had received before coming on this second excursion to Asilomar. I decided to follow the advice that was given to me. I determined that I will not try to go anywhere. I will listen to my inner guidance and allow myself to show up where I am supposed to show up.

I began just walking and thinking, letting what I was experiencing simply happen or unfold, without any expectations. I enjoyed looking down at the ground, up at the trees, or at people. If someone were to have noticed me, they might have thought that I was a tad bit inebriated, as I would let my legs and feet carry me wherever "they" wanted to go. I might walk to the left, and with the next step, go to the right, basically without any sense of direction or destination whatsoever. But believe me; I was far from being a bit tipsy.

Demonstration: My Boots

One of the topics for discussion at the Conference was creating our own demonstration. Please let me explain: Through the mental and spiritual activity of thought, directed toward a definite end, we bring about a greater good, a more abundant life, and a more joyous condition than existed before. This is called a demonstration. We can demonstrate at the level of our ability to know. The treatment which leads to the demonstration is not for the purpose of making something happen but is to provide an avenue, within ourselves, through which things may happen. Spiritual demonstration is the manifestation of Reality.

The first demonstration had to do with my boots... "My left boot now fits."

At that time, I had a pair of boots that had been in my possession for about six months. On the day I bought them, they were rather tight so I had to have them stretched. The fact of the matter is they had to be stretched again. I could wear them for only short periods of time because they were still a tad bit uncomfortable, so much so that my left foot would hurt every single time I removed the boots. I mean PAIN!

I did a treatment in the morning before putting on the boots that they fit me comfortably. I wore the boots all day and hardly knew that I had them on. For many years I continued wearing the boots and always in complete comfort.

Reflection on Consciousness and Aging

I was quite moved by what we were told at another presentation. The speaker was talking about a very large old tree in Pacific Grove on the Asilomar Grounds near the ocean. It was said to be unusual for the trees in that area to grow as old and as large as they do because of the unfavorable environment: the sand, heavy rainy season, and then extended periods of no rain at all. The speaker then uttered these words, in reference to the tree:

"You will not die as long as you continue to grow. When you stop growing in consciousness, you die."

The words were healing and seemed limitless in their nature. For me, there seemed to be a deeper meaning in those words than in anything that was said in the entire lecture.

"You will not die as long as you continue to grow."

Reflecting on these words, I began to consider a new way of seeing myself and others in a way that is free of the concept of age. It seems to me that we put far too much importance on age, dates, birthdays…which all reinforces the belief that we are not only going to die but that we expect to die. What would it be like to live without the constant belief that we are aging and on our way to dying?

I imagined, if we were to randomly select a group of sixty-year-old people and place them in a line, there would be those who look, speak and act as we might expect 60-year-old people to look and behave. In that same sample, there would be others who look more like they are 90 years old than sixty. Then, of course, there would be those who give the appearance of being much younger than their age, which is vivacious and eager to drink in life. These youthful ones love to dance, sing and laugh. They have a good time, enjoy themselves, have a drink, and make love!

Upon reflecting in this way, I received a profound lesson about life: How our life unfolds is always a question of mind over matter. It is not some hocus-pocus diet, miracle drink, or exercise routine. Our personal convictions determine who we are and how our life unfolds, and this can be seen in one's being, apart from our physical age.

Next time you are out and about, look at the people around you. But don't just look. Invite them into your consciousness. Understand them and be aware of who and what they are, but above all, listen. Chances are pretty good that some will show you how unhappy they are, how cruel and mean life is. They will complain that they can't do this and they can't do that. Even though the individual might not be conscious of it, that person is exactly who and where they have chosen to be. In essence, they are a victim of no circumstance other than the creation of their own thoughts.

On the other hand, look around and identify at this same function – be it a wedding, church function, funeral, or social gathering – one who acts and talks more like a child. A person who has this exuberance about them... a magnitude about them... a certain air about them... some would say an aura... a vitality. Talk with this person! Share yourself with them, and they will enjoy sharing themselves with you. In time you will be drawn always to the positive person, and let this person see themselves in your being. And, as they experience you, and you experience them, each will be reflected in the radiance of the other. It is so easy to experience the joy of life. It is so very, very easy.

Experiencing Self as Source

Tonight, before going to Merrill Hall, I shared with someone a few of the experiences that I had during the week. It was an exciting and humbling experience.

During the evening presentation, I was just sitting, enjoying being there when I had an urge to leave. As I was leaving Merrill Hall, I went down the steps and headed in the direction of the Administration Building. All of a sudden it was as if multiple voices, both masculine and feminine, simultaneously summoned me. They didn't call me by name but I felt I must respond to their invitation.

I increased my pace slightly, looking for the place I was supposed to go "I'm coming," I said out loud.

Again, I had the feeling of being called by the same voices.

I responded out loud with much more urgency, "I'm coming."

Then I started running, but I didn't know where to run. Tears were streaming down my face. Still, I heard no voice. There was just that feeling inside me, an urging. "Come here!"

"I'm coming!" I cried out loud, but still, I did not know where I was to go. It was incredibly exhilarating for me. I stopped running for a moment and then started walking, slowly looking in different directions, still not knowing where I was supposed to go, but assuring myself that I would know when I got there. I walked on and found that the ground was soft beneath my feet. This place was near the circle of trees and grass behind the administration building in front of the dining hall.

Suddenly, I knew this soft ground was the place. I dropped to my knees and cried. And I mean, I cried! Somewhere inside me, I felt very ashamed and humbled; not for crying, but in some way, for not thanking the Source for all that has been happening to me. In so many, many ways, much of which I cannot adequately express in words right now, I am so thankful for all the experiences in my life.

A deep, deep sense of humility overcame me. I just cried. I will never forget that experience as long as I live. I was apologizing for every thought I had to do something and didn't follow through and complete it—for every action that I planned and didn't complete, for every idea I had and didn't follow through on it. I was ashamed that I had all these actions that went uncompleted. I felt I should apologize to my Creator/Source as a son apologizing to his father. I was humbled and wanted to say how sorry I was and at the same time wanting to express my joy and to thank the source for these profound experiences.

Yes, I cried, because I realized that we all walk a path to bring us where we are... right now. If we had not ventured down this path, quite simply, we would not be here. And when this realization dawns on you, as it did for me this night, you are overcome with tremendous joy, gratitude, and humility.

I realized that I was simply opening up to the Divine. I composed myself and suddenly I had a vision of a beam of white light. I was moving horizontally on the beam of light. Then I realized I was the beam of light and the light immediately went vertical. The beam seemed to expand and as I looked at it closely it appeared to reflect light as it does when refracting off a quartz crystal. The beam was vast, flowing both up and down for infinity. The beam and I were one white, reflecting essence surrounded by a sea of black. The experience was beautiful and breathtaking. This experience wasn't physical – it was all taking place in my mind, but at the same time, I was definitely feeling the sensation.

I was there in profound joy, relishing the moment – when someone came up behind me and stepped on a twig. I was startled and felt a bit afraid and the vision evaporated in an instant. Once again, the feeling of having disappointed someone came over me. But as I look back on that experience now, I should have known better. What in the world could hurt me when I am in communion with the Source?

I remember saying to myself, "Where is my beginning? Where is my end?" What comes to me is, "Alpha and Omega." Even though I can't describe it in words, I know that it all makes sense. It was one of those "Oh, now I see" experiences. It was an encounter that opened my mind and allowed me to see, "seeing" in a whole new light. The invisible (that which is within) became visible. It had nothing to do with seeing "out there." But it had everything to do with seeing, with knowing, with feeling, coming in touch with ... "Oh! I See Now." I am forever. I have no beginning and I have no end. I feel warm inside, and that feels good.

Reflection on This Day

I got rid of ego and learned humility. I discovered my belief in love. My path of enlightenment is confirmed. These observations...these insights...are very personal and profound. We all choose our own path, although many people are not conscious of it. I realize what I want to be...what I want to do...and where I want to go this day. I know that I am where I need to be and that I am destined to be here.

The experience of this day was already unfolding in the most incredible way. Only two days into the conference, and already I know that this is going to be the best week of my life. As I went to bed, part of me reflected, "Indeed, today was absolutely tremendous! How could anyone experience a better day?"

As I drifted off to sleep, something in me knew that tomorrow was going to be even better. And...indeed it was.

CHAPTER 4

Day Three

In accordance with my insights of the previous day, I permitted myself to allow spirit to show up for me. I walked the grounds at every opportunity, following the direction of my inner voice. I wandered moving without reason to the right or the left, walking where my feet took me. I kept to myself and did not gravitate toward people who I knew at the conference as I did not want to get caught up in idle chit-chat. I made a point of not eating meals with anyone to maintain that same state of "being in the flow."

Most of this week I have spent alone by choice and the effects have been startling. For example, when I went into the Administration building to get hot chocolate or just to be in the presence of other people, I was thinking about something and then I heard what I was just thinking in conversation from people around me.

Encounters with people voicing what I had been thinking occurred all week. I was in this meditative mode all of the time, in solitude but never feeling alone as my thoughts were reflected back from everything around me.

I found myself to be very much at home in the woods. Whenever I got near a spot that I had previously visited, I felt very familiar emotions coming out again; the welling up of tears in my eyes and a deep sense of humility and a sense of spontaneity. Again and again, I was drawn to the same location. I felt like touching things ...mostly trees.

The Partner's Heart Workshop

I didn't go to very many workshops, but this one was profound. Everyone had to find a partner, and you took turns holding your hand over one another's heart. First the partners – in this case, my partner was a lady – were instructed to lie down on the floor. The facilitators came by and moved my hand to be directly over her heart. And then it was my turn. The lady put her hand on my heart. I could feel the warmth of her hand immediately. The facilitators took us through some type of meditation, and a cold sensation began to come over me. Initially, I could feel her warm hand, and then I couldn't feel it anymore. I began to have this cold and white (like turning into ice) working its way up my body.

The workshop ended, and I was aware of everyone leaving, but there were a few people that stayed and I was amongst them. I was just shaking and I could see my body was getting white moving up my torso into my entire body. Several of the facilitators came by and put their hands on me. The heat from their hands immediately dissipated the white sensation and my body got warm again.

I never understood what that was that happened to me. The facilitators suggested it might have been the beginning of an out-of-body experience.

I see people looking at me. I feel their presence. Yet I ask myself, "What's going on?" I have not done anything nor shared any of the experiences that I have had this week so that I might not attract attention. Yet people seemed to be looking at me.

The Power of Our Thoughts and Words

I am experiencing new highs every day, many, many times a day. The words Alpha and Omega keep returning to me. I ask myself, "What's going on? What does all this mean?" As I talk to people or even contemplate things within myself, I gain a clearer insight into these words as I become conscious of what I am saying and thinking. As I contemplated the words Alpha and Omega it was empowering. Alpha was on the left and Omega was on the right and I was in between. The I AM presence was in between the Alpha and Omega. It wasn't just me. It had to do with all humanity. Everyone has that power within themselves. I was recognizing the empowerment within me.

I find it important to remove negative or limiting words from my vocabulary. I must speak and think in a positive empowering way.

I received some interesting assistance in this endeavor. If I said, or even thought something limiting or negative, a light (so to speak), would flash in my mind, and a voice would say to me, "Do you know what you just said?" It would then simply be a matter of restating or rethinking the thought in a positive and supportive manner.

This still happens to this day. I know this is successful because I can literally feel the difference in my body, which is then followed by a tingling and other sensations that let me know that what I have just thought or said is in some way limiting... not supportive or empowering of myself.

To take this a step further... When I say or think something that is empowering to me, it just is and that is all that matters. It is also expected (when I say something that is limiting to me in some manner) that I will always receive this awareness or sensation. This is usually followed by the question, "Do you know what you just said or thought?" This causes me to say or to rethink things in a more constructive and empowering manner.

Another wonderful day! Again, it works! Today is grander than yesterday in many ways. The knowledge grows!

CHAPTER 5

Day Four

I felt a need to thank some of my guides and teachers, so today I sent flowers to a couple of them and phoned one person. To the rest, I said thank you in my mind. As a result of, and in response to, the special events and occurrences that I experienced at the beginning of the week, I am spending a great deal of my time in somewhat of a meditative state. All of my walks, or strolls, if you will, have been at a noticeably slower pace than before coming to Asilomar. (This still continues for me today, some twenty years later.) I realize that there is more going on in my life than I can physically see or experience. It is indeed multi-dimensional. At the same time, I realize and I know that I am contributing to the whole of humanity in everything I think, do and say.

Recollection

Today, for no apparent reason, I suddenly started crying and did not know why. I thought back to the experience of being the white beam of light and in that instant remembered a similar vision that came to me about six months ago. That experience was absolutely wonderful! The light was infinite. It went on forever. It was just incredible! And it was not that I was on the light, or next to the light, I was that light. I also had this feeling that people were looking at me and the number of people was increasing at a rate I could not comprehend.

At that time a few months ago, I was afraid of the responsibility that one assumes in being that beam of light. But today, I suddenly realize that now I am no longer afraid and that is what all of the tears are about. I know that other people have had a similar experience. What it comes down to is everyday life! Right now, dealing with our kids, cooking dinner, shopping, working, in a relationship, whatever, we don't have to be afraid of who we are.

The Tree Branch

As I approached Merrill Hall today, I was continuing to walk slowly. The doors were open allowing me to hear the speaker. I was late arriving and could hear the speaker inside the building beginning his presentation. A moment before each word was spoken; I knew what was going to be said. I listened to about three sentences and I light-heartedly said to myself, "Well I guess that I know all of that, so I don't need to be inside."

I got back into my meditative walking mode and slowly wandered behind Merrill Hall, zig-zagging back and forth and circling around Merrill Hall where the ground and vegetation meet the roadway. I walked near the edge of the road circling back towards Merrill Hall, looking at the ground and after what might have

been three-quarters of an hour or so, I found myself approaching a pine tree with a branch that was about eye level.

As I slowly approached the branch, I lowered my head slightly and reached out with my hand, and gently raised the branch so that I might walk under it. The moment I touched it, I instantly started to cry. Not just a cry but a loud bellowing sob with tears streaming down my face and I did not know why. Passing slowly under the branch, reaching behind me, I let go of the branch and stopped crying, instantly. "WOW!" I thought. "What's going on?" All of a sudden, I was overcome with an incredible rushing sensation. I turned around and grabbed the branch and held it for a while, trying to recreate what had just happened. I tried this several more times, but nothing happened. I turned around and walked back in the direction of Merrill Hall, but decided once again, not to go in and listen to the speaker, but rather I chose to think about and digest what had just transpired when I touched the tree branch.

Experience of the Fog

After my experience with the branch, I sat down on the opposite side of Merrill Hall about 40 feet from the building attempting to contemplate what had just happened. I was distracted by the voice of the speaker.

After sitting for a while, I got up and walked in the general direction of the dining hall. I walked past the boardwalk that leads to the ocean and a short distance I saw an embankment that was to the left of the walkway. I settled down under a tree near the boardwalk and began to contemplate while sitting under this tree. I wondered out loud, "What in the world is going on? I have had one seemingly unexplainable thing after another happen to me all week!"

I stopped talking to myself and began to notice my surroundings. A thick fog was closing in around me. Soon a gentle mist began falling. From where I was sitting, I could see the tall blades of grass next to me bend over due to the weight of the moisture that was falling. I thought to myself, "What a marvelous experience this is, to be sharing and to be experiencing this sharing, or if you will, this gift of nature, rather than sitting inside Merrill Hall listening to a speaker."

I spent several minutes taking it all in. After a while, I noticed something strange. Here I am sitting in what to some would most certainly be a cold, damp, wet fog. I look around me. "I should be shivering," I whisper to myself, "But I am not, I'm warm." I look at the drops of moisture on the bent-over blades of grass dripping next to me and between my legs. I look at my clothing. "I'm not wet at all!"

Not only was I not wet or cold, but I was in fact warm! It was as if I was sitting on a heating pad. I reached underneath me and felt the ground. It was dry. I touched my clothes all over and I was not wet, yet the grass was bent over dripping wet all around me. I wept. (And even as I share this with you now many years later, my eyes are welling up with tears.)

I sat under the tree for some time. Eventually, my tears dried. I looked ahead at the Administration Building. Suddenly, the white fog seemed to be moving to the right. I could feel the wind blowing on the back of my neck in the direction of the Administration Building. But yet as I stare at the white fog it is moving from my left to my right. I blinked and suddenly the fog was moving directly from my rear toward the Administration Building.

Tears welled up again with this experience in wonderment. The experience happened again multiple times. I could come up with no explanation as to what happened and perhaps this is as it should be. Why try to explain or document what had happened, when all I need do is revel in the feeling of wonderment and humility.

Years later, I realized that what I was seeing with the movement of the fog was part of my own aura.

Hugging a Tree

After some time, I got up and started walking. I resumed my slow, meditative walk. As I neared the faintly defined Chapel, a man walked up to me through the fog and said, "You should go hug a tree. Nature wants to communicate with you." He looked me in the eyes, smiled, turned, and walked away. I realized that everyone else was at Merrill Hall except this one person, and he had walked up to me. He had spoken to me. As I watched him fade into the fog, I stood there in wonderment and humility and wept again.

Later that day, I did hug several trees but I felt somewhat self-conscious, thinking "What if someone sees me?" I looked around to see if anyone might be in the area to see me. As I hugged the trees, I did not feel anything in particular and experienced nothing out of the ordinary. After several hugs, I realized that what I was doing – determining to hug trees and see what happens – was out of the flow of what this week has been…being in the flow and allowing things to happen, without trying to make them happen. Realizing this, I understood that nature is already communicating with me and I refrained from hugging any more trees during this Asilomar visit.

Food for Thought

I slept in this morning, and then after taking a walk, I found myself in the lunch line. I remembered I didn't have my lunch ticket with me. Immediately, the lady in front of me turns around and says, "Oh my, I asked for another lunch ticket and now I have two tickets" and so she gave me a ticket. I was standing in line, realizing I wasn't hungry. So I decided to step out of line and eat only when I was really hungry. I didn't eat again during that experience at Asilomar. I was never hungry, I never even thought about food.

Mysterious Feathers

As I continued my slow, meditative walking back around the grounds I saw many feathers. I now chuckle at this, having seen the movie Michael. These were light gray and I saw a lot of them on the ground while I was walking around. I was contemplating the abundance of feathers on my walk. As I slowly walked through the Administration Building, along with several hundred other people, I looked down at the floor and saw many more grayish-white feathers similar to the ones I had seen earlier. I looked around to see if there was any reason for this and could find no explanation.

Evening Calling

At around nine in the evening, I was sitting in Merrill Hall listening to the speakers. Even though I was listening, something was telling me to leave the hall. At the time, I had no idea why I was having this feeling because I was really enjoying the presentation. Be that as it may, something was pulling at me, was definitely trying to get my attention. After so many unexplainable things had happened that week, I knew that I had no choice but to give myself to this notion and leave.

As I walked, I felt I should head toward my car and kept asking myself, "Why in the world am I walking to my car, when there is nothing that I really need or want in my car?" No sooner had I uttered the question to myself when I came upon an older gentleman who could not stand up. He was collapsed along the right-hand side of the road almost across from the administration building. From the look on his face, I could see that he needed some assistance, and I also knew that he had not been drinking. I approached him and asked if he was all right.

"I am so very tired and fatigued." He paused. "I was supposed to ask for assistance but I didn't want to be a burden to anyone." His eyes swelled up and tears fell.

"He said I should not be walking, but..." He looked up at me. "But I wanted to leave Merrill Hall before everyone else so that nobody would see me struggle to make it home."

I told him to just sit there on the ground and I would get my car and take him home. As I headed for the car that sensation that I had been experiencing so many times overcame me again. Now I knew why I left Merrill Hall! (Even as I am sitting here recalling the incident, tears are again coming to my eyes.) There I was, the only person out at this time of the evening, except for this gentleman who required some assistance.

I drove him home and helped him into his house or the place that he was staying.

My car was parked off-grounds because I had arrived late not trying to be anywhere at any particular time. There were perhaps 800 people at Merrill Hall as we were well into the evening presentation. I thought I would look for a closer parking place. And there for my pleasure was the closest legal parking space to Merrill Hall.

Again I had one of those Aha! Moments that put a smile on my face. I was parked probably the furthest from Merrill Hall and because of being in the flow, I had the closest parking space.

I entered and went to the very back of the hall. Reflecting on this amazing evening, a very warm, comfortable feeling remained with me as I watched the last of the evening's presentations.

Vision Corrected

The evening program was well underway and I was seated in the very back of Merrill Hall listening to the speaker. Normally throughout the week at Asilomar, I did not carry my glasses with me as I am nearsighted and my vision wasn't so that I needed my glasses for driving. I mostly just left my glasses in the car, I had somewhat of a comfort zone wearing them when I was driving, so I rarely carried them with me.

This particular evening, I wanted to see the speaker and I put my glasses on, and to my astonishment, I could not see the speaker at the front of Merrell Hall. I flipped my glasses up away from my eyes and looked straight ahead and I could see everything perfectly. I did this repeatedly looking with and without my glasses at the speaker. In my astonishment, I could see the speaker clearly at the front of the auditorium without my glasses, and with my glasses on everything was distorted at the front of the auditorium.

I realized again in my humility another change this week and that my eyesight had miraculously corrected, and once again the tears flowed as I embraced this marvelous happening.

CHAPTER 6

Day Five

Ask and It Shall Be Given

As I walked the Asilomar grounds, especially when I was in a relaxed state of mind, I found that whenever I would ask myself a question, the answer would always present itself. These answers would be given to me in different ways. For instance, I might ask myself something, and within moments, someone would approach and start talking about the question I had just posed to myself.

I remember reading that all answers come forth from within us – perhaps this is the explanation. But now, as I give this notion some more thought, I realize that in asking a question, a void is created, and the universe is poised to respond from any number of sources. It was astounding! I wondered if I was psychic to what was going to be spoken next or if the universe was responding to my query.

I sat down in the afternoon on the steps behind the Administration building. A lady was playing the guitar, while other people were coming and going. I listened to her music for 45 minutes to an hour. She looked up and said what a pleasure it was to play for me, how the music just flowed for her. She had never experienced the feeling of eagerness to play for someone that she got playing for me. I listened to a few more songs, thanked her, and then continued my walking.

In that instant, I realized that I had absolutely no desires. I was perfectly at peace. I know this because I felt it. I was touched by it. It is the nature of the Divine to be touched... to be felt.

In fact, a lady introduced herself and said to me, "Your face is shining. There is a light around you." I was quite humbled by this and I didn't know what to say to her. I noticed the sunlight shining and I said to her, "The light is all around us." I ever so humbly continued my meditative walk.

Discovering the Meaning of Sustenance

Thursday evening after the presentations, I was walking around in a meditative state, walking very slowly, not really going anywhere, keenly aware of what was going on around me, free of any particular desires. I had a bag of pretzels with me, and I had eaten several of them. After a bit, I started remembering excerpts from a book I had recently read, The Life and Teachings of the Masters of the Far East, by Baird T. Spalding (Available from www.devorss.com). In this fascinating book, he refers to the Masters being able to sustain themselves for many days on just a few grains of rice. I remember asking myself, "How can that be?"

That was all I needed to do, simply ask the question. I had a piece of pretzel in my mouth that I was just breaking off. It was between my tongue and the roof of my mouth. As I broke off the pretzel, I had a sudden rush of energy going from my tongue down the front of my body and from the roof of my mouth up to my head and down the back of my body. At the same time, I could see my whole body three-dimensionally in front of me, and I could see a grid system throughout – the grids going vertically were about five times thicker than the ones going horizontally. The grid system was lit up three-dimensionally in gold right in front of me and I could see the energy as it passed from my tongue to my toes and to the tips of my fingers. It was just incredible to not only feel but to be able to see simultaneously what was happening as this energy moved through my entire body!

All of this happened in a mere fraction of a second. The people walking nearby did not see the vision. I paused in awe of what had just happened. I was continuing my meditative walk towards the dining hall and saw a raccoon near the trash can. I no longer desired the pretzels and left them on the ground for the raccoon.

The vision lasted only a fraction of a second but has stayed with me for the rest of my life.

After returning home, I went out and bought the largest bag of rice I could find. I think it was twenty-five pounds. For years I kept it in my home. Even to this day, I keep a container of rice on my counter. Sometimes I stare at it and contemplate my experience. I can visualize that there is enough rice to sustain me for quite a long period of time if I find myself again in that consciousness.

The Alpha and Omega

This evening, I was attending a motivational lecture on self-worth and positive thinking. I was standing at the time, and to the best of my recollection, the realization of Alpha and Omega came to me at the conclusion of the talk: Alpha in my left hand, and Omega in my right hand. Alpha is the beginning, and Omega the end. We all have this essence within us and we are the infinite that is between Alpha and Omega.

CHAPTER 7

Day Six

"Yet another lesson awaits me today. What's next? My excitement is overwhelming."

I found myself in line at lunch after the bell rang and contemplated that I wasn't hungry. Often, we automatically eat despite not being hungry. Pondering this and accepting that I was not hungry; I stepped out of line and decided I would eat again when I was hungry.

Divine Dining

I just wanted to walk and take in, or digest, what was going on around and within me. But in the evening, I got dressed for dinner. I was standing in line when I realized that I still wasn't hungry. There I was, standing in line, and for what reason, I didn't in fact know.

I decided to feast my eyes on the people standing around me. I was amazed at how structured they were. Every day of the conference, three times a day, there they were standing in line. But this Friday night's meal was a bit different. It was the last night of the conference and many people were dressing up in their evening gowns, suit coats, and ties for dinner. I did not want to go in and just sit there since I still was not hungry.

Then it dawned on me. The morsel that I was seeking suddenly came to light. I was given some more insight as to what had happened to me the night that I had my encounter with the pretzel.

Let me assure you, I had no intention of bringing this on myself. As a matter of fact, for several days, I had asked myself, "Are you hungry?" And the answer I would always get is, "No, I am not hungry."

I believe in metaphysics and I also believe in the power of the spoken word. As I have learned from the Ernest Holmes material, it is important to become conscious of what you are saying, for in many cases it speaks to what you carry in consciousness. In this light then, it is also important to keep in mind the law of right action... as it pertains to the question, "Am I hungry?" Initially, I told myself, "I am not hungry." I realized if I said, "I am not hungry." I was setting up a scenario, if you will, within my own body, commanding it not to be hungry. So, I determined that any future thoughts would be expressed "I'll eat when I'm hungry."

The word "not" has no place in the law of mental equivalent and correspondence. Simply stated, the limit of our ability to demonstrate depends upon our ability to provide a mental equivalent of our desire, for the law of correspondence works from the belief to the thing. But it is within our power to provide a greater mental equivalent through the unfolding of consciousness and this growth from within will finally bring freedom.

When you say and feel "I AM," you release the spring of Eternal, Everlasting Life, to flow on its way freely and unmolested. In other words, you open wide the door to its natural flow. "I AM" is the Full Activity of the Divine.

When you say "I AM not," you shut the door in the face to this Mighty Energy. Every time you say "I AM not," "I cannot," "I have not," you are, whether knowingly or unknowing, limiting this "Great Presence" within you. Using the words, "I AM not," you still set in motion Mighty, Limitless Energy, which continues to act unless it is recalled and the imperfection consumed and transmuted.

With this truth in mind, I removed the word "not" from my vocabulary and my consciousness. It is not a matter of my not being hungry, but rather knowing that I AM satisfied and fully nourished and sustained. Let's just call this food for thought and leave it at that.

The Stump that Couldn't Be Reached

It is 1:30 p.m., and I am enjoying my slow, meditative sojourn in the woods on the Asilomar grounds. I feel... I AM limitless. All I need is before me. I am glad to be back in nature. As I walk, I think of my friend, Betty who told me over and over again to take the time to smell the flowers. I am realizing that there is more to it than, shall we say, smelling the flowers. I remember another friend telling me the significance of the sense of smell. One who is knowledgeable and wise in the ways of the world and spiritual or metaphysical teachings is said to have a nose for knowledge. With this thought in mind, I now realize what Betty meant. She was telling me that one of the most important attributes of one who is wise and knowledgeable is one's willingness and ability to listen.

I was walking in the woods and was remembering Reverend Betty telling me to listen to all that surrounds me, especially my guides, those who are looking out for me and directing me. All I need to do is listen and know that everything happens when we are ready.

As I walked further into the area, I looked at a stump that was a little way in front of me. A beam of sunlight was falling directly on the stump.

It did not take me long to realize that sitting on that stump in that beam of sunlight was where I wanted to be. I approached the stump several times from different angles, but no matter how hard I tried, I could not get to that stump. There were obstacles in the way that prevented me from completing my mission.

At one point, I took a step and immediately sank about a foot into the tall grass. The grass seemed to wrap itself around my ankle as if to hold me back. So, I had to stop for a moment and contemplate what was happening. I started feeling a bit silly, and for whatever reason, somewhat guilty.

I realized that was the first time during the entire week I was actually trying to go somewhere. Initially, I was out for my usual meditative kind of walk, but somewhere during the stroll, I decided that I was going to attempt to "control" the walk and the meditative state. My regression into controlling my experience was not working for me, as was evidenced by the fact that I could not get to that stump. The ground was not wet or swampy, nor was there a ditch in my path. It was just tall grass... about two feet high and very, very dense. Plus, it was a new crop of fresh grass. Again, no matter how hard I tried, I could not navigate my way through it. I approached the stump again from another direction and my second step brought me into a mucky swamp. It was obvious, I couldn't continue in that direction.

Indeed, the same could be said for the meditative state that I wanted to achieve. I just could not control or direct it either. So, for all intents and purposes, I could not go where I wanted to go. I had to go where "it" was going to take me. Clearly, that was the essential message of the entire week.

Oak That Wishes to Be Undisturbed

It seemed to me that the tree stump wanted to be left alone that day, so I let my intuition guide me. I slowly walked a bit more and was led to yet another tree stump; this one seemed to welcome me with open arms. The stump was partially covered with vines of poison oak. I reached down and gently moved the poison oak over so I could sit on the stump. I sat down and let the sunlight pour down on me and began to take in my surroundings. The most noticeable landmark, other than the stump that I was sitting on, was a deer trail on the ground right in front of me.

I noticed a lot of poison oak all around me. There was a time when I might have not even gone near the plant, but as I realized my Oneness with All That Is in and around me, I simply removed the word from my consciousness. I said to myself, "This plant is just oak that wishes to be undisturbed." As I began to take a closer look, I noticed that the entire area was covered with this plant. I realized that I had definitely walked through the foliage and brushed up against it... my pants, boots, shirt, and even my arms. I meditated for some time and basked in the warm sunlight. I returned the poison oak to its place on the stump and continued my slow, meditative walk around the grounds. Contemplating this whole scenario with the poison oak, it should be noted that I didn't get one itch.

Last Night in Merrill Hall

Many people did not want the experience to come to an end. In line with what I expressed in my initial prayer treatment, I am convinced that this Conference Experience is indeed meant to be lived. It is meant to be taken with you... to be savored and lived every day for the rest of your life.

It was the last night at Merrill Hall. I was seated on the right-hand side about 2/3 toward the back of the room. I gazed around the room and made eye contact with people looking at me again. I didn't understand why they were looking at me. I wasn't wearing anything conspicuous. I wasn't doing anything that would demonstrate anything but humility.

And suddenly I wanted to speak. It was the same feeling – I re-member it quite clearly to this day – when I got up and left Merrill Hall those previous nights. I wanted to get up and speak, and I thought "how outrageous of me" and I contemplated "what would happen if I got up?" My body was trying to get up. I grabbed onto the chair and got white knuckles while I was holding myself on the chair as I sat listening to the speaker. With all my force of will, I resisted the urge to get up from my chair.

To this day I still wonder about that impulse that seemed to wish to speak through me, and in what ways my life would have been changed had I chosen to surrender at that moment. I had no idea what I would say. Would I have made a fool of myself or have said something enlightening? At times I regret that I didn't speak. That was the only time during the week that I didn't follow my inner direction.

Evening Adventures in Monterey

Friday evening after all of the activities were concluded, I was full of energy and quite high. I didn't just want to go home and go to bed, so I decided to head to Monterey. I stopped by the Brass Rail, a lounge on the top of the DoubleTree Inn. I enjoyed listening to the entertainment and asked a lady to dance. It was a slow tune but it was a song I really loved with a bit of a beat to it. It was "Sailing" by Christopher Cross.

Immediately when we began dancing, other couples started bumping into us. I thought this to be a bit unusual, for rarely does this ever happen to me, plus I was watching where I was leading the lady. I felt like a ball in a pinball machine, bouncing back and forth and back and forth, sometimes twice at the same time from two different directions. I would guess we were bumped into over thirty times in that one dance. After the dance, my partner apologized to me and said, "I am so sorry about all of the bumpings into us, but, for some reason, it seems to happen to me every time I dance."

"That explains it," I said to myself. As she walked away, I wished that she might question why such things were happening to her. She was clearly unaware of the fact she was creating the situation by speaking about it, and in fact, expecting it to happen. But, be that as it may, she did not ask, and I knew that it was not my place to offer an explanation without her asking.

The band began playing another similar tune so I asked another lady to dance. Once again, the dance floor was full. I closed my eyes and didn't just dance in one place, but I deliberately moved about the dance floor with her, even twirling the girl around a couple of times. Not one person bumped into us, and we did not bump into anyone either.

The Acquaintance with Colorful Language

After the dance, I was silently contemplating this example of how we create our reality when an acquaintance of several years came up to me and started talking. I had known this person to be one who tended to use what I shall call "colorful" language. He was very animated, speaking fast, talking of our supervisor and his managerial skills in a loud and aggressive manner, using profanity every time the opportunity presented itself, which frankly was quite often.

Staring at him, I took a deep breath and spoke the words "I love you" softly to myself about 25 times as he spoke the next three sentences. He gradually calmed down and began to speak slowly and softly without using any profanity. I have come in contact with the individual several times over the years and he has always been very pleasant to talk to and has never used profanity again in my presence.

The "Heavy Metal" Bar

I left this lounge and went outside across the street, where I could hear loud heavy metal music coming from a lounge on the second floor. I had never been attracted to this kind of music in the past but it seemed that something was certainly drawing me to that place on this particular evening.

I walked upstairs and stood in a line to pay my cover charge. I said hello to the person checking IDs and taking the money. She returned my greeting but didn't ask me for any money. So, I wished her a pleasant evening and entered the lounge. A person was taking the cover charge receipts and stamping the back of people's hands. In the past, I had left establishments because people insisted on stamping me. The individual greeted me; I returned the greeting and walked into the room. He never asked me for my payment receipt nor did he want to stamp me.

The room was filled with people, some standing… some dancing. I noticed an empty table on an elevated area on the far side of the room. From this vantage point, one could view the entire room, dance floor, and the band. It was indeed a special location. It was very possibly the best table in the house. As I approached the table, I thought it a bit odd that the room was full of people and yet that one table was unoccupied, seemingly waiting for me. I took my seat and began surveying the surroundings. I enjoyed listening to the music and watching the people, an exercise that in the past I would have judged and perhaps avoided altogether. The band leader and other band members nodded their heads to acknowledge me shortly after I sat down at the table. I nodded and returned their greeting. Others also seemed to be glancing at me.

Some people at the table next to me were smoking clove cigarettes. In the past, I had found it to be an offensive fragrance. I would have judged not only those who were smoking but what they were smoking as well. But on that night, I realized that all I had to do was breathe through my mouth and not my nose. I didn't smell the cloves at all. I said hello to these people and ordered a bottle of beer and cold glass from a waitress. As my drink was brought to me, I noticed that people were looking at me. And I say again, I was really enjoying people watching and appreciating the fact that I was in no judgment of what was going on.

Several minutes passed, and then someone made their way out of the crowd and was walking by my table. It all seemed to happen in slow motion. The individual bumped into my table. I could see the bottle of beer, the glass, and an ashtray all sliding down the tilted table towards me. Suddenly, the folks at the table next to me came to my rescue. They jumped up and caught all three items before they tumbled into my lap. I thanked them and wondered to myself if they would have been so eager to help me had I judged them.

Later that evening, I returned to the Asilomar Grounds and spent several hours pondering the events of the day.

As I take the opportunity to look back over the week's activities, I realize that every day... every hour... was what I must call one of those "Oh, I See Now!" experiences... an incredible opening of profound personal awareness. This once again leads me to affirm:

I choose to live the life that is intended for me

and I choose to live it to the fullest.

CHAPTER 8

Conference Last Day

Four days after my encounter with the pretzel, I still have no willful desire to go on a spiritual fast even though I have not eaten for several days. I have no desire for food whatsoever.

Conference Summation Gathering

Finding myself in Merrill Hall for the Grande Finale of the week, a recap so to speak, with a slide show presentation of mostly the speakers but also many of the attendees. A pleasant way to reminisce as you contemplate your enlightening week of lectures, workshops, and experiences.

One slide after another would fade in and out of view with the various speakers and attendees. As inspiring music filled the room, I noticed my picture amidst these grand presenters. My eyes swelled up wondering why they had my photograph on the slide presentation. After a few more slides of other people, there I was again. Before the entire slide presentation was over various shots of me appeared perhaps 5 or 6 times. I couldn't contain the tears streaming down my face. It was a profoundly humbling experience for me.

The Universe Responds Again

On Saturday, I was walking alone on one of the walkways and, as usual, looking at the ground continuing my slow, meditative walk. I was smoking at that time in my life. It was quite a leisurely stroll and I was thinking about public speaking. I had this little

"thing" about public speaking because I really did not want to get up in front of a group and speak. I remember thinking "Who am I? There are so many others who are more qualified. I am just myself, what business do I have... what authority do I have to speak to a group of people?"

I love to talk and share personal experiences. That, I suppose, is a key for me. Rather I simply share my experiences from a personal perspective. And it means a great deal to me when, in sharing these experiences, I can contribute to another person's feeling of greater self-worth.

Be that as it may, I would even get goosebumps just thinking of public speaking. I stopped walking for a moment and took in the surroundings when a man walked up to me and asked me for a light for his cigarette. I gave him a light, and he thanked me.

After lighting his cigarette, the gentleman said to me, "My life has certainly changed since I became involved in the Toastmasters and got over my fear of public speaking." He told me how warm, helpful, courteous and very constructive they were. He went on to say that they never criticize but rather are empowering.

I thanked him for sharing and he went on his way. As he walked away my eyes swelled up as I remembered myself "How can I overcome my fear of public speaking?"

There I was walking and thinking about all of the wonderful experiences that I had during this week at Asilomar. And when I looked up, there was this guy, who, without me asking, provided the answer to the question that I was pondering. I just shook my head amazed and I continued my meditative walk.

CHAPTER 9

The Journey Continues

Synchronicity of Lights

Departing Pacific Grove, to visit my friend in Salinas, California, I noticed on arrival, that every single light had been green. The only time I stopped was on my arrival at his home. Salinas is one of those cities that had at that time motion-activated stop lights rather than synchronized stoplights. Normally, you could hardly make two lights without stopping. Even on my return to my home in Camarillo, I was free of intersections with red lights.

The Power of "I Love You"

On the way home from Asilomar, I stopped by a friend's house to say hello. He was not home, but his cat was outside in the courtyard. Normally, this cat would have nothing to do with me. I said hello and the cat paused. I said to the cat, "Don't be afraid."

The instant I said the word afraid the animal got up, ran through the courtyard, then across the lawn, and scrambled under a car. I went up to the door and rang the bell. When it was evident that no one was home, I turned and started to leave. I saw the cat looking at me from under the car.

This time I tried a different approach. I spoke softly. I removed the word "afraid" from my vocabulary. I spoke only positive words saying, "I love you and I know you love Me." repeatedly. The cat immediately moved out from under the car and came over to me. He allowed me to pet him and then he nuzzled me and rubbed against my leg.

Just one of those things that happened, you say? Come to whatever understanding you wish for yourself. To my way of thinking, it was another marvelous revelation of the power of the words that you speak. Get rid of negative words in your vocabulary, and every word you utter will be an affirmation of empowering truth. Once I took the words of fear out of what I was saying, the cat wasn't afraid.

My Return from Asilomar

So, I returned to my daily life after this extraordinary experience. I did not eat a thing for over three weeks. I did have liquids, but no solid food at all. I had stopped saying that I am not hungry. I would say to myself that I will eat only when I am hungry. I began to get frightened as I thought no one can go over three weeks without eating. Although I still was not hungry, I made myself a can of soup and slowly ate it. For many months after this, I ate only a piece of bread and a bowl of soup to keep my body nourished.

Upon my return from Asilomar, I found that I no longer had the desire to consume hard liquor and have not done so since. When I ordered my first bowl of soup at a restaurant, I ordered a glass of red wine for the first time.

The effects of the experience transformed my life in many ways in that I learned how to function in a meditative state all the time. I could be at work in my corporate job, in a bustling crowd of people, and maintain a slower mental pace. I seem to remain calm in stressful situations that would have upset me in the past.

For instance, when my computer crashed I remained unruffled, where before my Asilomar experience, I would have been frustrated and angry. I find now that if I make a wrong turn while driving, I just calmly make corrections rather than becoming angry. In the past, when there were several customers on hold and the phone lights were flashing impatiently at me, I would feel the pressure. Now, I calmly take each call without worrying. I notice that now if my car breaks down, I simply think that I will get it fixed, rather than getting upset over the inconvenience.

Recently, as I opened the door of my refrigerator, the door fell off spewing the contents on the shelves all over the floor. I had absolutely no reaction. I was calm and free of emotion or anxiety.

As I contemplate the absence of intense reactions to life situations, I recall a time that a minister had invited me to attend a drumming workshop. I declined to explain that the noise made me uncomfortable and elevated my blood pressure. She said, "Of course, you are accustomed to being in a more quiet meditative state." She did not make me feel guilty for not participating. She acknowledged my needs without judgment.

My body lets me know when something is disharmonious. For example, I have noticed that low bass notes cause me extreme discomfort. I am aware of a shift in the "energy" when certain people enter a room. I experience many occasions now where I can see my aura. When I look through my aura, all objects passing by will appear to be the color of that portion of my aura. It is a fun way to pass time watching people and/or automobiles changing from one color to another as they pass by.

Synchronicity in My Corporate Job

In my corporate job, I was a produce buyer. I would do phone work first thing in the morning to find out what was available and the current market prices. Then, with this information, I would contact my customers to receive and then to fulfill their orders for that day and throughout the week. This particular morning, the broccoli market, which closed the previous day at $4 a carton, was already $5 and $6 and going higher. I called my customers to let them know they should give me their orders for the week as soon as possible. I then continued my other activities. I finished my procurement duties after about the first 2 hours that morning.

More than three hours into the morning, I answered the phone in a happy, jovial way, referring to "the organization's finest" – meaning me. My customer said, "You won't believe what I need." I interrupted him and said, "Whatever you want, you've got it!" He then proceeded to say, "I've got to have a load of broccoli [meaning a semi-trailer load of broccoli] shipped today." I said again, "You've got it!" I hung up the phone and remembered that this particular customer was the first person I alerted regarding the rapidly rising broccoli market. I hung up the phone and the next inbound call was from a broccoli shipper offering me a load of broccoli. I asked him what the price would be and he answered saying that the market was very active but the market yesterday closed at $4. "Let's leave it at that". I didn't even make a phone call to place the order – they called me and offered me the broccoli at the precise time I needed it, and at yesterday's prices!! At that time, I would have paid as much as $11 a case, which was the high market price, to cover the order.

Uncovering My New Name

My first name was Howard. Some people used to call me "H." I had always wanted to change my name, even as a child. As a teenager, I recall wanting a different name, and this thought was with me through my early thirties.

But what name? Each time I thought about a name change, I would say the traditional male names but nothing would ring true for me.

A couple of weeks after the Asilomar experience, I was reading a book about Egypt and the Pharaohs and how they would have Ra in their name. Finally, I knew I had part of my new name! I was so happy! I have wanted for so many years to have a new name and now I had a piece of it. I had tingles all over and was smiling from ear to ear. I could not remember a time of such happiness in my life. After some time and consideration, I added the word "man" to "ra." Initially, I didn't know if "ra" was the front, middle, or back of my new name. I would introduce myself to new acquaintances as Raman and feel the waters of it, as it were. I didn't tell any of my existing circle of friends of my desire to change my name. This was just between me and my new acquaintances. After a month or so, I stopped doing this and went back to using my given name.

Sometime later, I attended a channeling session in someone's living room, and a person asked the channeler for a more spiritual name than the one they were given when they were born. The channeler gave her a new name and then half of the participants raised their hands asking for a new name. After responding to those wanting new names, the channeler looked right at me and said, "The reason you haven't changed your name officially is you're still missing a piece." He spoke directly to me, although I didn't have my hand up. I looked around, to see if he was speaking to someone sitting behind me. There was no one there. I pointed to myself and nodded my head. He continued: "The name you've chosen is masculine, but you are looking for balance. The letters "da" in several languages are feminine and if you put it on the back of the name that you have chosen it will give you the balance that you seek." So now all of the pieces had come together, Ra-man-da. For me, it meant "god/man balanced."

I changed my name legally two weeks later, and Ramanda has been my name ever since.

The Violet Flame

At another Asilomar conference several years later, I was standing near the back of Merrill Hall, leaning up against one of the posts that support the balcony. The speaking had ended for that session and people were departing. At this point, there were two to three hundred people still in the room. Looking out over the crowd from the back of the room, not looking at any one person, in particular, I saw this violet flame. It was perhaps 40-50 feet away from me, at least 10-12 feet tall and 6-8 feet wide. It was a little to the right from the middle of the room.

I stood there motionless in awe looking at the flame, and I heard a male voice say, "Do you accept?"

No one else seemed to notice the voice or the flame even though they were walking all around it and through it.

I didn't respond right away because I was pondering what had just happened. The voice repeated, with authority, like calling your child the second time with more urgency, "Do you accept?"

I said "Yes!" and immediately the flame came right at me and when it reached me, everything in the room that I looked at turned violet- the people, the chairs, the ceiling, walls, floor, everything.

This experience has stayed with me all these years. I think about it almost every day.

It has been said that the Violet Flame is the union of the pink light of the Divine Feminine and the blue light of the Father God. As such, it represents Oneness, the whole. I am allowing the meaning of this to unfold from within me.   It was because of this experience with the Violet Flame that I decided to use the color violet in the text of my publications.

Visions of Violet

At the most recent Asilomar conference, I was at Crocker Hall (the banquet hall). I prefer to sit with my back near the wall, so as not to have ambient chatter all around me. I was sitting in front of the fireplace, wearing a violet shirt and looking out over the room, smiling from ear to ear.

I saw a lady in the middle of the room wearing a garment the same color as the shirt I was wearing. As I looked out over the room, she caught my eye repeatedly. It wasn't that she caught my eye; it was the intensity of vibrant violet around her.

I decided to go over and compliment her on her stunning wardrobe selection thinking we had chosen the same color on that day. I headed out into the middle of the room and as I got to within about 15 feet of her, the violet disappeared and I realized she was wearing three or four colors and not violet. I saw the brilliant violet around her repeatedly after I returned to my seat.

I went about my day then, just walking the grounds (I don't attend workshops anymore and rarely stay for lectures in Merrill Hall). I arrived at Merrill Hall at the end of the session and was leaning against a pillar that supports the balcony. I remembered the experience that morning of the lady with the violet aura that I thought was a garment. Should I tell her I was seeing her aura? I said to myself, "Well if she comes by, I will tell her." I no sooner had that thought and there she was passing in front of me. I followed her outside the building and I tapped her on the shoulder. I told her the story, how I had admired what she was wearing across the room that morning because our colors matched. She looked at my shirt with a puzzled look on her face, as I explained that it wasn't her garment I was seeing, it was her spectacular violet aura. She threw her arms around my neck, hugged me, and said, "Thank you, you've made my day!" and we each went about our activities.

Later that afternoon, I was standing near the same pole of the balcony near the back of Merrill Hall. As a lady I recognized walked by, I said, "That's a great color on you!" She thanked me and she walked out of the hall. A few minutes later, I glanced at her. She was outside and the coat she was wearing was a brownish-orange but when she had previously walked by me, that coat appeared to me as a dark violet. The next person that walked by seemed to be wearing a brilliant yellow. Not only could I see but I could feel that it was a perfect color for that individual. As she passed by I told her that the color looked great on her. As she walked a few steps away, the color faded away and I could see the actual color of her garments were dark; not even near yellow.

After this experience, I said to myself, "I should stop complimenting people on the lovely color of the garments they are wearing. "To this day, I hesitate to comment on the color someone is wearing.

I've seen violet many times, and since this Asilomar experience, it's been even more intense. I see shades of violet over everything. It seems that many times when I relax my eyes, I see violet.

Mission Ranch, Carmel, California

Sunday, November 23, 2008

Sitting at the bar sipping a glass of champagne, listening to Gennady, the piano player, I was motionless and staring out through the window, perhaps thirty feet away, at the beach, sand, ocean, and the hills in the distance.

My view began to change as everything that I was looking at slowly faded away, along with the dark green ceiling beams and wood above the windows. The view was changing to white, kind of like a fog at first, and then reflected white light back to me. Tables, chairs, serving tables, windows and people faded from view. Staring at this for some time, I started to notice the colors red and dark blue in my peripheral vision.

When I turned my head in the direction of the colors that I was seeing, I saw people as they would normally be seen, without any colors around them. I looked back out the windows and in just a fraction of the time that it originally took; the white reflection of the haze/fog began again. Several more times, I would see colors in my peripheral vision and each time when I turned my head and looked directly at the person, the colors were gone and I saw only their normal appearance.

After several attempts of turning my head to see the colors, I was seeing to the right and the left, I was keeping my head straight, looking out the windows with my eyes fixed on the beach and ocean in the distance in front of me. After several moments, the view in front of me became mostly all white, the people walking in front of me and those to my right and left were dark objects without features, with color around part of the dark shadow. I realized I was seeing part of the auras of everyone in the room. In some cases, I only saw the color or colors to the right and left without the dark silhouettes in the middle. The colors or combination of colors were white, red, pink, rose, orange, light and dark green, light and dark blue, light and dark purple, and yellow/gold.

This experience lasted for several minutes. It stopped when humbled by the experience, emotion started to come over me and my eyes began to tear. I was joyous, in awe, and humbled all at the same time. Wow! I spent the next several hours in quiet contemplation slowly walking the streets of Carmel.

My Dear Friend, Mission Ranch

December 8, 2008

At Mission Ranch listening to Gennady playing the piano, as I stared at a singer, I slowly began to see translucent to dark violet in my view over everything. I turned my head to the right and I looked through the windows into the night darkness.

From my stool in the corner, my view, without a conscious effort, filled again with translucent to dark colors of violet, with light to dark red in the middle. My eyes teared as I listened to the song, "The Impossible Dream" that Paul was singing.

At the conclusion of the song, I wiped away the tears from my eyes and looked back in the direction of the people around the piano, grateful that my tears went unnoticed. I walked over by Paul and as I thanked Paul for singing, he wiped tears from his eyes and explained that as he was singing that last song, he was thinking of his friend Scotty and that he had sung that song at the party honoring Scottie for acquiring his Ph.D. and again at his memorial service. I hugged Paul, thanked him again, and went outside to be alone, and to shed some more tears, remembering my dear friend.

CHAPTER 10

Reflections

My goal is to meditate every day. I say many affirmations; these are a few that are always included:

The source and I are one

I am Christ consciousness

Joyous synchronicity fills all aspects of my life

I contribute to the forward thrust of the

consciousness of humanity

With joy, I release these words,

knowing that as I have spoken gratefully,

so it is.

CHAPTER 11

My Gift to You

These stories I have offered are subtle affirmations of your future... of everyone's future. Every time such words are uttered or thought, this action contributes to the expansion of the consciousness of humanity. We are forever part of the whole. I know it. I feel it with every word I speak and with every breath I take. What we think ...is. What we speak ...is and forever shall be.

I can't help but smile when I think of this. I get one of those body rushes every time I say, "I Am." Try it sometime. Next time someone says to you, "Hi. Are you having a good day?" ... instead of saying "Yes," "No" or "I don't know..." Whatever mood you're in, respond by saying, "I Am!" See if you don't feel better. See if it doesn't give you a tremendous high, and a rush! When that happens, know that you can continue building on that rush, any time you choose. That high is all around you. Just open up your eyes and look!

As each one of us grows in our awareness of who we are, we are contributing to all of humanity. Each one of us is important. We are important in that we have a relationship to all others.

What we do and say is important. The people we connect with touch other people. There is no doubt in my mind that when I meet people and, after spending some time together, I leave a little something behind! As I do this, I grow in my awareness. I say that with all humility. I enjoy making others feel happy and shed some positive light in their lives. It gives me such a rush. It is wonderful... the most exhilarating force that I feel.

While walking on one of my first boardwalk experiences at Asilomar I remember saying hello to someone. That was the first time that I could truly feel that connection when I said and smiled hello. It was unlike all of the many previous times in my life I said hello to someone. On this occasion, and many times since I felt and I knew that there was a connection. In the past, greetings were mostly without feeling or emotion. At Asilomar, I began to look forward to greeting people, reliving the joy and connected experience of the moment.

It is within our power to be remembered positively or negatively. Whatever we are radiates. I prefer to think that everyone wants to be positive! If you want to know what you truly want in life, look at what you have right now. Your subconscious mind is responsible for most of your experiencing and your learning. What is happening in your life right now is based on what you are thinking, but not on what you are thinking consciously. There may be subconscious programming present that limits your ability to fulfill yourself through action.

But here's the secret: allow yourself to become conscious of that which you truly are. Become aware of the I AM presence that is experiencing itself in and through you right now. Just relax and allow yourself to experience the truth of your Being.

I know the Christ Consciousness is within me, waiting, wanting to express, to come forth, just as it is in you. I am like anybody else, and this plays a large role in my desire to help other people. Christ Consciousness is perhaps asleep within you, but if you desire IT to come forth, IT will. Simply speak the words, the door will open. The original writing of this book took some twenty years. I tried many times to listen to the audiotapes or review my notes. I would immediately start crying; for the emotions of the experience would come right back in the same manner as they did when the actual events happened. And I must say such is the case today.

What I have shared with you on these pages is most profound and personal. I know that the nature of all things is to move forward. I am living in the present, and as I reflect upon these shared experiences, it is my sincere desire to contribute to the empowerment of the consciousness of humanity. And as I do, I encourage you to do as the U.S. Army slogan reads "Be All You Can Be". I fervently believe this is the way all of us can live our lives every single day. It is our individual choice how we experience the next moment.

You are a thriving, pulsating artery in the consciousness of humanity and I offer these affirmations for your opening to your I AM Presence:

I affirm my Oneness with the Source.

Right now I know I Am.

I Am on an evolving, developing path that continues propelling me always forward.

I Am awakening to the qualities and attributes that are my true nature, contributing to the forward thrust of the consciousness of humanity.

I am living in ecstasy right now.

My future is now and forever.

That which I desire already IS.

I Am forever joyously one with the Source.

I thank all those who have helped and guided me and with profound humility and great joy, I release and know that as I have spoken these affirmations, so It Is!

Namaste

Consciousness

Ever since I had the magnificent week at Asilomar in 1985, I have desired to live in that consciousness every day 24/7.

Meditating: Mostly while I was walking slowly amidst nature, repeatedly affirming; I am one with source, I am Christ consciousness, joyous synchronicity fills all aspects of my life...... (sometimes I add things like; I am one with nature, I am happy and joyous) I never just sat and meditated per se, one of my takeaways from this week at Asilomar was what I call active meditation. I slow down my walking and my thinking. I would state my affirmations slowly with each step. Even when I was with or around other people, if I wasn't actively involved in their conversations, to myself I would repeat my affirmations.

Here are the major contributors to that marvelous week. Living the consciousness of...

Gratitude

Profound humility

Emotionality

High expectations

Being amidst nature

Relaxed, happy, respectful, and sincere. I always enjoyed being in the company of other people.

Walking slowly all day as though everything was slow-motion in my world.

Being in the flow. Allowing myself to be wherever I was supposed to be at that particular moment, never trying to get someplace or be on time. I attended very few events and the ones I did attend I generally arrived late and frequently left early.

Followed my intuition

No TV, news, texting, or cell phone

Minimal decaf coffee

Minimal alcohol

CHAPTER 12

Afterword: One Religious Science

One element of interest to me was working to combine RSI (Religious Science International) and UCRS (United Churches of Religious Science). First, let me give you a little background. The movement known as Religious Science or Science of Mind was founded in 1927. Years later, in 1954, due to difficulties in the approach to incorporate structure and church administration, the member churches chose to create two organizations to perpetuate the teachings of Ernest Holmes, the founder of Religious Science. The two organizations were united in the purpose of helping people become more aware of the principles and techniques of Religious Science so that their lives may be enriched.

In perusing the works of Ernest Holmes, I believe that what Ernest Holmes wanted future generations to understand (because those around him already knew) was that the Church of Religious Science was not a product of his ambition. He saw the origin of the church as a virgin birth. It had no earthly father, no external cause. Consciousness was its genesis. Once the child was born, for which he took no credit, he welcomed its appearance and embraced his role to nurture, inspire, and give counsel. He watched it grow beyond his expectations. He cherished the organization. The ministers were his colleagues – every one of them. He was at their beck and call day or night. He was devoted to the welfare of every church, large or small. He treated for each one of them. He envisioned their success, imagined their prosperity, and visited them with parental affection. But the church was not born out of the wants or needs of Dr. Ernest Holmes. He did not see himself as anyone's guru.

The church literally gave birth to itself. It was a spiritual happening, an evolutionary awakening in community after community. He never took credit for that, not because of some false modesty or feigned self-effacement, but because he believed he was merely a conduit, a vehicle for a higher expression of consciousness, appropriate to his time and place. As he would say, it could not have been otherwise. He was grateful to be that instrument, and his denial of a desire for a faithful following or some pious recognition was genuine. It is a noble gesture, a quality of humility that comes from wisdom derived from metaphysical insight and internal honesty.

So, in this context, it is true that Dr. Ernest Holmes never set out to found a church. He had no such religious ambition or theological craving. But once the church was born, he loved it with every fiber of his being and gave it everything he had.

When I arrived home after my awesome experience at Asilomar, I collected the addresses of all the Centers of Religious Science using the Creative Thought magazine (of the International Centers for Spiritual Living) and Science of Mind (from the United Centers for Spiritual Living). I composed a mailgram and sent it to every Center of Religious Science. In reading it, they affirmed that there is one Religious Science.

RSI and UCRS continued to be separate for several years and reunited to form what is now Centers for Spiritual Living in 2006. All those years ago, I affirmed and put into the law of Right Action that they are One. RSI and UCRS do not hold any meaning to me anymore. There is only one unit, and it is Religious Science. It is not Religious Science of New York or Boston. There is one Religious Science – as Dr. Holmes intended.

ABOUT THE AUTHOR

Ramanda is a modern-day mystic, author, teacher, lover of nature, and a way-shower. He founded Reflections of Divinity (a spiritual non-profit) to illuminate his personal transformation into readable and relatable stories for anyone seeking the revealing of their inner awareness – their divinity.

He started his retail career in the seventh-grade selling gift wrap and candy for schools, and at the age of 16 began his 28-year career with Jewel Food Stores. During his tenure with Jewel, he held many positions including managerial, quality control, and buyer.

His determination and positive outlook continued to serve him throughout his life. Ramanda served two years in Vietnam receiving several citations and offered a field commission.

His marriage of five years ended after his wife succumbed to an illness, leaving him to raise their two small children.

Ramanda started a non-profit, Reflections of Divinity, assisted a motivational speaker, created motivational media, produced several televised programs on public broadcasting, and is the author of two books.

His newest book - The Spiritual Awakening of H - is a story of his spiritual awakening. It is written in an authentic, heartfelt, and inspirational manner offering readers an opportunity to examine their own lives.

ramanda@reflectionsofdivinity.com

Made in the USA
Columbia, SC
14 September 2021